▶● Contents

Any words appearing in bold, **like this**, are explained in the Glossary.

About the experiments and demonstrations

In each chapter of this book you will find a section called 'Science Answers'. This describes an activity that you can try yourself. Here are some safety rules to follow:

• Ask an adult to help with any cutting using a sharp knife.

• Magnets can spoil tape recordings. Do not use magnets near videotapes or audio cassettes. Magnets can also distort the colours on a TV screen, and the distortion may not go away.

• Never connect the two terminals of a battery directly together – the large current could burn you.

Materials you will use

Most of these activities can be done with objects that you can find in your own home. A few will need items that you can buy from a hardware shop. You will also need paper and pencil to record your results.

What is magnetism?

A **magnet** is an object that acts in special ways. It pulls some objects towards itself, and it pushes some others away. These effects are called magnetism.

If you can find a magnet at home or at school, you are bound to find them fascinating. You can test what sorts of things are attracted to magnets. There is something eerie about the way they can push and pull each other across empty space without touching each other.

Switched-on magnet

This crane can lift metal objects, using magnetism instead of a hook. The magnetism is generated by an **electromagnet**, a type of magnet that works with **electric current**. The magnetism can be turned on and off by turning the current on and off.

SCIENCE ANSWERS

Magnetism

EDUCATION LIBRARY SERVICE

Browning Way
Woodford Park Industrial Estate
Winsford
Cheshire CW7 2JN

Phone: 01606 592551/557126
Fax: 01606 861412
www.cheshire.gov.uk/els/home.htm

Heinemann
LIBRARY

www.heinemann.co.uk/library

Visit our website to find out more information about **Heinemann Library** books.

To order:
☎ Phone 44 (0) 1865 888066
▤ Send a fax to 44 (0) 1865 314091
▥ Visit the Heinemann Bookshop at www.heinemann.co.uk/library to browse our catalogue and order online.

First published in Great Britain by
Heinemann Library, Halley Court,
Jordan Hill, Oxford OX2 8EJ,
part of Harcourt Education.

Heinemann is a registered trademark of
Harcourt Education Ltd.

Editorial: Sarah Eason and Georga Godwin
Design: Jo Hinton-Malivoire and
  Tinstar Design Ltd (www.tinstar.co.uk)
Illustrations: Jeff Edwards
Picture Research: Rosie Garai
  and Liz Eddison
Production: Viv Hichens

Originated by Ambassador Litho Ltd
Printed and bound in China by WKT

ISBN 0 431 17493 8 (hardback)
07 06 05 04 03
10 9 8 7 6 5 4 3 2 1

ISBN 0 431 17501 2 (paperback)
08 07 06 05 04
10 9 8 7 6 5 4 3 2 1

British Library Cataloguing in Publication Data

Cooper, Christopher
Magnetism. – (Science Answers)
538
A full catalogue record for this book is
available from the British Library.

Acknowledgements

The Publishers would like to thank the
following for permission to reproduce
photographs: Corbis **p. 28**; Corbis/James
Leynse **p. 8**; Corbis/Lester Lefkowitz **p. 20**;
Corbis/Michael S. Yamashita **p. 10**;
Corbis/Stephen Frink **p. 26**; Gareth Boden
p. 22; Imagebank/Getty Images/Marc
Romanelli **p. 21**; Liz Eddison **pp. 7,
15, 18**; Photodisc **p. 29**; Science Photo
Library/Jeremy Walker **p. 5**; Science Photo
Library/John Howard **p. 23**; Science Photo
Library/Martyn F. Chillmaid **p. 9**; Science
Photo Library/Pekka Parviainen **p. 25**;
Trevor Clifford **pp. 6, 11, 14, 16, 24, 27**;
Tudor Photography **p. 4**.

Cover photograph of a collection of
magnets reproduced with permission of
Tudor Photography.

The Publishers would like to thank
Robert Snedden and Barbara Katz for
their assistance with the preparation of
this book.

Every effort has been made to contact
copyright holders of any material
reproduced in this book. Any omissions
will be rectified in subsequent printings
if notice is given to the Publishers.

Magnetism is at work all around us – in all kinds of machines and appliances. Magnetism is vital to the working of **loudspeakers**, telephones, radio and TV sets, computer disks and **electric motors**. In factories **motors** drive lifts and cranes. In the home they power appliances such as washing machines and vacuum cleaners. In cars they power windows and remotely controlled door-locks. All these motors depend on magnetism.

What sort of magnet have I got on my refrigerator?

The sorts of magnets that you use to hold notes on the side of a fridge are called permanent magnets.

Inside the plastic or ceramic cover is the magnet itself. The magnet is described as 'permanent' because it keeps its magnetism, provided it is not heated too strongly and does not receive too many violent blows. The magnet and the iron or steel of the fridge attract each other, so the magnet is held to the fridge. They can even attract each other through the thickness of a few sheets of paper placed between the magnet and the fridge. However, the more sheets of paper that are added, the weaker is the attraction.

▶◦ What do magnets do?

You can do lots of interesting things with one **magnet**, and even more if you have two.

Try the effect of moving a magnet next to a pile of metal paper clips. The magnet will pick up a lot of them. The paper clips are pulled towards the magnet. We say that the magnet **attracts** the paper clips. Magnets attract other magnets and some other materials. Paper clips are made of steel. Steel is attracted to magnets – we say it is **magnetic**.

The paper clips cluster around the ends of the magnet, but hardly at all around the middle. The places where the magnetic **force** seems strongest are called the poles of the magnet. The pattern of these forces in the space around the magnet is called the **magnetic field**.

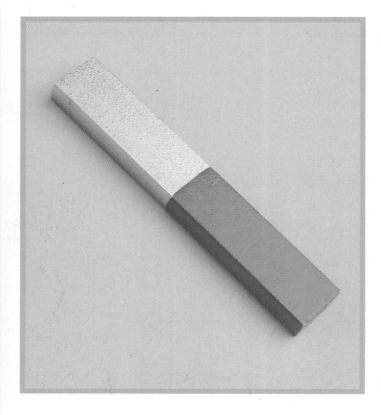

Can I get one magnetic pole by itself?

A magnet is often bar-shaped, and is then called a bar magnet. If you could cut a bar magnet in half, you would end up with two magnets, each with two poles. A new pole would appear on the newly cut face of each magnet. You could keep cutting the magnet again and again, each time producing two new poles. A single **magnetic pole** is never found on its own.

Horseshoe magnets

A horseshoe magnet is like a bar magnet that has been bent to bring the two poles close together. This is just because, when you are using the magnet to attract things, it is convenient to have all the pulling power in one place. Horseshoe magnets are mostly used for toys or for school science demonstrations.

Keeping things tidy

In homes and offices magnetism helps to keep small metal objects from getting lost. These paper clips are being held in place by a small magnet.

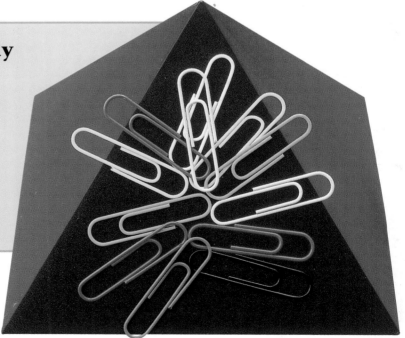

Different poles

The two poles of a magnet are different from each other. Hanging the magnet by its middle so that it can turn freely can easily show this. After swinging to and fro for a while, it will come to rest with one pole pointing north and the other one pointing south. The same pole will always point north. The north-pointing end is called the magnet's north pole; the other end is called the south pole.

Can magnets push as well as pull?

Two magnets will behave differently depending on which poles you put closest to each other. If you have two bar magnets, you will find that the two north poles **repel** each other (push each other apart). The two south poles also repel each other. The north pole of either magnet attracts the south pole of the other one. In other words, like poles repel, unlike poles attract.

A smooth ride

Powerful magnets on this train and on the track repel each other. The train hovers above the track, giving everyone a smoother ride.
This train is called a **maglev** train, because it is levitated, or raised, by magnets.

EXPERIMENT: What shape is the magnetic field of a bar magnet?

HYPOTHESIS:
Magnetic forces are strongest around the poles of
the magnet.

EQUIPMENT:
A bar magnet, some iron filings from a hardware shop,
plain paper.

EXPERIMENT STEPS:
1 Place a sheet of plain paper over a bar magnet
   (prop the paper up at its corners so that it lies flat).
2 Gently sprinkle some
   of the iron filings onto
   the paper.
3 What happens? Draw a
   picture of what you see.

CONCLUSION:
The filings cluster around
the poles of the magnet
and form curved lines
running from each pole
to the other one. They
show that the effects of
the magnet make a pattern
in the space around it.

The pattern of magnetic
effects around a magnet
is its magnetic field. The
lines are called field lines.
The iron filings make the
field visible.

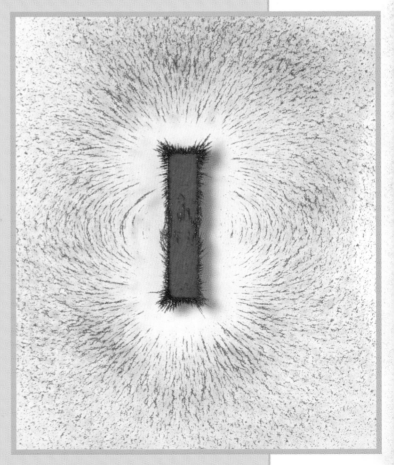

What sorts of things are attracted to magnets?

Scientists call a material **magnetic** if something made of that material is either a **magnet** or can be **attracted** to a magnet. Iron is magnetic. Steel, which is mostly iron, is also magnetic. Most metals are magnetic.

Although a steel paper clip is magnetic, it is normally not a magnet – it will not attract another paper clip. If a magnet is held close to it, not only is the clip attracted to the magnet – the clip itself becomes a magnet, attracting other clips. You can see this by dipping a bar magnet into a packet of paper clips. You can pull out a whole lot of clips, with the ones at the bottom clinging to the ones higher up, which cling directly to the magnet. When you remove the magnet, the clips lose their magnetism and do not cling to each other.

Recycling

Magnets can be used to separate iron and steel objects, such as pieces of scrap, from objects made of non-magnetic materials such as **aluminium**. The iron and steel can be recycled for many different uses.

EXPERIMENT: Why are some objects magnetic?

HYPOTHESIS:
Some household objects are magnetic because they contain iron and steel.

EQUIPMENT:
A bar or horseshoe magnet, a variety of household objects.

EXPERIMENT STEPS:
1 Test household objects by seeing whether a magnet attracts them.
2 Try pins, needles, paper clips and cutlery.
3 Try similar things made of different materials – paper, wood, plastic, other metals.
4 Try different sorts of coin.
5 Make a table of your results. Which things were magnetic?
6 Find out what sorts of materials the magnetic things were made of. Ask adults, or try to find out in books and on the Internet. Write the results in the table.

CONCLUSION:
You should have found that the items that were attracted to your magnet were all made of metal. Most are made of iron or steel, but some may contain other magnetic metals, such as nickel.

▶• What causes magnetism?

Magnetism exists because of the way matter is built. The matter in the things around us, and even in our own bodies, consists of tiny **particles** called **atoms**. Atoms contain several kinds of even smaller particles, including **electrons**.

The magnetism of a permanent **magnet** is the result of combining the magnetism of all its atoms. And the magnetism of each atom comes from the magnetism of the electrons in the atom. Each electron acts like a tiny magnet. In an atom most of the electron 'magnets' point in opposite directions. Their magnetism largely cancels out, but not completely.

Is everything magnetic?

Nearly every substance is weakly **magnetic**. This means that if it is placed near a **magnetic pole**, it becomes weakly **magnetized**. But it is magnetized in such a way that it is pushed away from the pole. However, this magnetism is so weak that only scientists working in a laboratory can detect it.

Iron, steel and some other metals, including nickel and cobalt, are different. When placed near a magnetic pole they become strongly magnetized, and are pulled towards the pole. When they are removed from the **magnetic field**, they may still keep some of their magnetism.

How do things lose their magnetism?

Magnetized objects can lose their magnetism. If they are heated sufficiently, or if they are knocked hard, their magnetism weakens. Magnets used in science and industry are made of special materials that lose very little magnetism when this happens to them.

Why is iron different?

A piece of iron is made up of tiny areas called **domains**. All the 'atomic magnets' in a domain are lined up pointing in one direction. The atomic magnets in the next-door domain point in a different direction. When the material is placed in a magnetic field, more and more atoms swing round to line up with the field. If the atoms in a domain are already pointing the 'right' way, that domain grows. Domains with atoms pointing the 'wrong' way shrink. As more and more atoms point the right way, the iron becomes a stronger and stronger magnet.

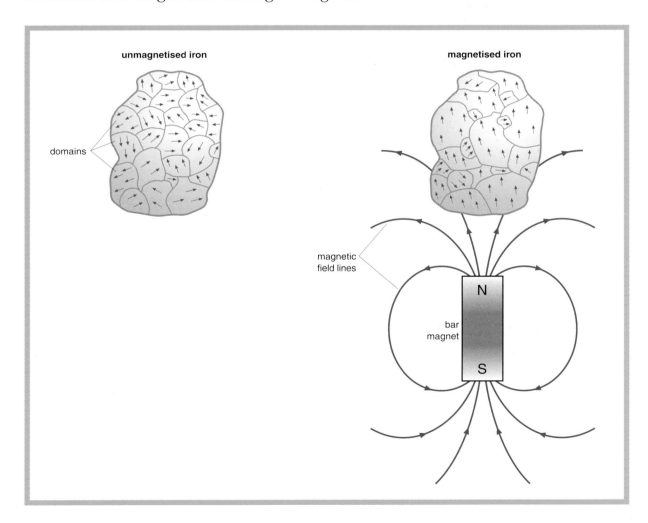

DEMONSTRATION: Making a magnet.

Magnets can be made from objects that contain iron or steel. Make your own magnet by following the steps below. You will need: a long iron or steel nail, or similar metal rod, a bar magnet and some metal paper clips.

DEMONSTRATION STEPS:

1 Check that the nail is not already magnetized – see if it will pick up the paper clips.
2 If it is not already magnetized, stroke one pole of the bar magnet along the nail repeatedly, always in the same direction.
3 After doing this about 20 times, see whether the nail will pick up paper clips.

4 Write down what you saw.

EXPLANATION:
The bar magnet **attracted** the atomic magnets in the nail and swung them round to make one strong magnet.

How can we turn a magnet on and off?

An **electromagnet** works only when an **electric current** is flowing through it. This is useful because it means that the **magnet** can be turned on and off by turning the electric current on and off.

How is an electromagnet made?

Every electric current creates a **magnetic field**. If you were to trace the **magnetic field lines** you would find that they are circles around the wire.

An electromagnet is made with coiled wires, not straight ones. The wire is coiled into a series of loops (called a coil or a solenoid). The field lines run along most of the inside of the coil and then come out at or near one end. They re-enter the coil at the other end.

The stronger the current and the greater the number of coils, the stronger the field, and the stronger the magnet.

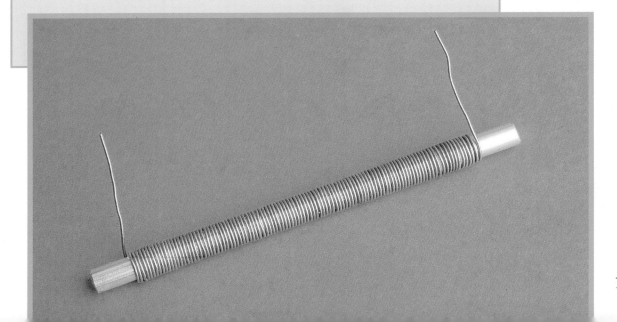

DEMONSTRATION: Making a magnetic force.

An electric current running through a coil will create a magnetic force. To demonstrate this, you will need: a large iron nail, from about 7 to about 15 cm long, about 20 cm of electrical wire, a **battery** with flexible contacts, some pins or metal paper clips.

DEMONSTRATION STEPS:

1 Trim about 2 cm of plastic covering off each end of the wire. Twist one end around one contact of the battery.
2 Twist the wire around the nail, making as many coils as possible and making them as tight as possible.
3 Hold the nail over the metal objects and touch the free end of the wire to the second contact on the battery. The current will flow and the nail will become an electromagnet and should pick up some of the metal objects.
4 Try more turns of the wire if necessary. If you feel the wire getting hot, take the end away from the battery contact for a while.
5 Write down what you saw.

EXPLANATION:

The magnetic field of the wire coil **magnetizes** the iron nail. The field of the nail is added to the field of the coil, making the electromagnet more powerful.

What can electromagnets do?

The most basic use of **electromagnets** is for pushing and pulling. Electromagnetic cranes are used in factories for lifting objects made of iron, steel or other **magnetic** metals. They are useful in scrapyards too, where they can separate objects made of magnetic materials from those made of non-magnetic ones.

You will find many things that use electromagnets in your home and at school. They are useful because we can turn them on and off. They can also be much stronger than permanent **magnets** because the more coils there are in the wire, the more powerful the magnet is. Electromagnets are a vital part of the **motors** used in washing machines, vacuum cleaners, computer disk drives and air-conditioners. They are needed in radios, TV sets and telephones. Outside the home, electromagnets open and close the sliding doors of shop entrances and lifts.

How can magnetism make sounds?

A **loudspeaker** turns **electric current** into sounds. The current comes from a device such as a **microphone**, CD player or TV set. The current passes through an electromagnet inside the loudspeaker. The electromagnet shakes the loudspeaker's **diaphragm**, which is a cone-shaped piece of metal or plastic. The shaking makes sounds, because sounds consist of **vibrations**, or rapid movements, of the air.

How does remote locking work?

In cars, electromagnets operate remotely controlled door-locks. When the driver sends a signal from the remote control, equipment in the car sends electric currents to electromagnets in the locks. The electromagnets move bolts inside the locks.

How do motors work?

Because an electric current has a **magnetic field** it exerts a **force** on a nearby magnet – it will 'try' to make it move. In return the magnet exerts a force on the wire carrying the current. **Electric motors** are based on this. In a motor a magnetic field makes current-carrying wires move. The diagram shows a simplified electric motor.

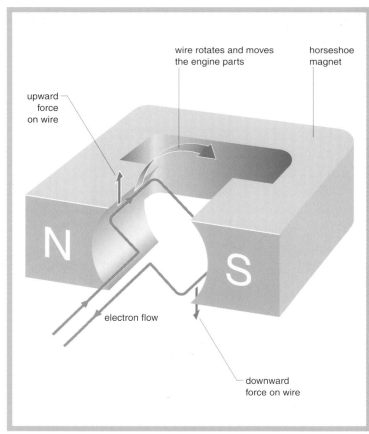

wire rotates and moves the engine parts

horseshoe magnet

upward force on wire

N

S

electron flow

downward force on wire

Magnetism in a doorbell

An electric doorbell contains an electromagnet. A visitor pressing the doorbell button pushes two metal contacts together, allowing an electric current to flow through the electromagnet. In one sort of doorbell, this pulls a metal 'clapper', or hammer, on a spring, hitting the bell. The movement of the clapper at the same time makes a gap in the **circuit**, switching off the current. The clapper immediately jumps back to its starting position, and the current flows again. The process repeats itself, and the clapper hits the bell again and again for as long as the visitor presses the doorbell button.

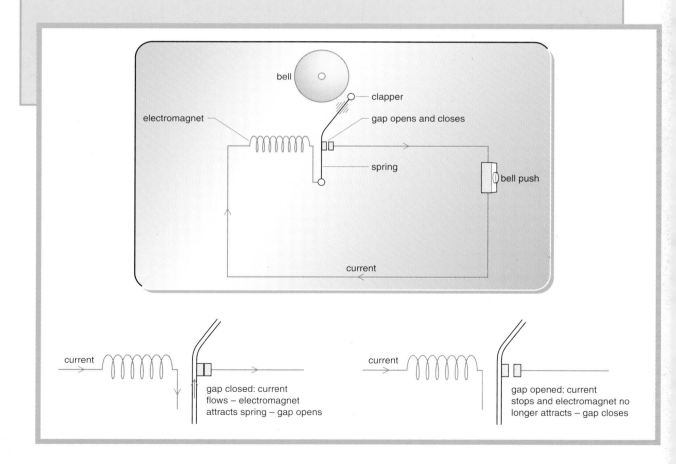

Can magnetism make electricity?

Just as an **electric current** generates a **magnetic field**, so a magnetic field can generate an electric current. A magnetic field can generate a current in a wire if it changes in strength – if it gets stronger or weaker. It can also generate a current if it moves, or if the wire moves while the field stays the same.

How can magnetism be used to make electricity?

A **generator** is a machine that produces electricity. It contains a rotating part, or **rotor**, in which there are coils of wire. The rotor turns inside other coils of wire. In **power stations** steam usually turns the rotor. Wind or running water can also be used to turn generators to make electricity.

Before the generator starts to work, a small electric current is sent through the non-moving outside coils. This makes the outer coils act as an **electromagnet**, producing a magnetic field in which the rotor turns. Because the rotor turns in the field, a current flows in the rotor.

Most of the current flows through electric wires to our homes, schools and offices. But some is sent to the generator's non-moving coils to make the magnetic field stronger, so that still more current is produced.

Changing voltage

Electromagnets are a vital part of machines called **transformers**, which make electricity safe for use in factories, offices and homes. Electric current is carried over long distances from the power station at high **voltage** (voltage is the 'push' that makes the current flow). The current flows to **substations**, where transformers convert some of the current to a lower voltage for use in factories. Other current is converted to a still lower voltage for use in homes.

Playing safe

A hand-held computer game does not need very high voltage. Electromagnets built into the machine reduce the voltage of the electricity from the mains.

What makes the Earth's magnetism?

The centre of the Earth is called its core. It consists mostly of iron, with some nickel. The outer core is **molten**, because it is extremely hot: 4500–6000 °C (8100–11,000 °F). The inner core is even hotter, but is solid because of the huge weight of the overlying rocks pressing down.

The molten outer core acts like a giant **generator**. The rotation of the Earth causes **electric currents** to flow in the molten iron. The currents generate the magnetic field that makes a compass needle point north–south.

What is the aurora?

In the night sky displays of shifting, ghostly coloured light can sometimes be seen. They are seen frequently in the far north and south, and so are called the northern or southern lights, or **aurora**. Electrical **particles** coming from the Sun produce these sky displays. These particles are affected by the Earth's magnetism. They travel towards the Earth's magnetic poles and collide with **atoms** in the atmosphere, producing light – the aurora.

DEMONSTRATION: How to make a compass.

You can make a simple compass by following the steps below.
You will need: a needle or long, thin nail; a permanent
magnet; a cork or some balsa wood; a bowl of water.

DEMONSTRATION STEPS:

1 **Magnetize** the needle or nail by stroking it repeatedly
  with the magnet. This will be your compass needle.
2 Now it needs to be attached to something that will float.
  Cut out a piece of cork, or a piece of balsa wood. Tape
  the needle to the top of this.
3 Now float it in a bowl of water. It will always turn to
  point north–south.
4 Write down what you saw.

EXPLANATION:

Your magnet acts as a compass, with one end always
pointing to the north.

Can living things sense magnetism?

Many animals have a '**magnetic** sense' that tells them the direction of magnetic north or south. In their bodies there are special cells containing **crystals** of the iron mineral magnetite. The crystals act as compasses, turning to line up with the Earth's **magnetic field**. Nerve signals from the cells carry this information to the animal's brain.

How long-range is the magnetic sense?

Mole rats dig tunnels up to 200 metres long, aided by their magnetic sense. When young, newts use their magnetic sense to find their way to their home pond from distances of as much as 15 kilometres. However, birds and many ocean-dwelling species **migrate** distances of thousands of kilometres, using the Earth's magnetism, and other clues to guide them.

Guided by magnetism

Loggerhead turtles nest on the coast of Florida, in the south-eastern United States. When young ones hatch, they swim out to sea and begin a five to ten-year journey 13,000 kilometres clockwise around the Atlantic Ocean. Laboratory experiments have shown that the Earth's magnetic field guides them.

EXPERIMENT: How can we show the effects of the Earth's magnetism?

HYPOTHESIS:
We can imitate Earth's magnetism by making a model.

EQUIPMENT:
A small bar magnet, some modelling clay, a small compass.

EXPERIMENT STEPS:
1 If you do not have a convenient bar magnet, you can use a short nail or other metal rod, **magnetized** as described on page 14. Press it into the centre of a ball of modelling clay.
2 Move the toy compass around near the ball to see the direction of the magnetic field.
3 Notice:
   a) how the angle of dip varies over the surface
   b) where the **magnetic poles** are
   c) where the magnetic equator is (needle not dipping towards either pole).

4 Write down what you saw.

CONCLUSION:
The angle of dip is different on different parts of Earth's surface. Migrating animals could use this as a clue to their position.

People who found the answers

William Gilbert (1544–1603)

William Gilbert was the personal doctor to Queen Elizabeth I and King James I, and was the first person to realize that the Earth is a giant **magnet**. He performed many experiments with **lodestones**. Studying how a **compass needle** behaved near a spherical lodestone convinced him that the Earth is a giant magnet. He wrote the first great English scientific book – the abbreviated form of its long Latin title is *De Magnete* (*The Magnet*). Gilbert invented the term '**magnetic pole**'. He was one of the earliest English scientists to believe that the Earth and planets went around the Sun. He believed, wrongly, that magnetism holds the planets in their paths around the Sun. He also studied electricity and clearly realized its differences from magnetism.

Hans Christian Oersted (1777–1851)

The Danish scientist Hans Christian Oersted was the first to find the long-suspected connection between magnetism and electricity. Oersted made his great discovery during a lecture to students in 1819. He was moving a **magnetic compass** near a wire carrying an **electric current** when he noticed a slight turning of the compass needle. He went on to study the **magnetic** effects of the current on all kinds of materials, and showed that the current was truly producing magnetism. His discovery created a sensation among scientists. As a result, within a few years others had discovered how to make the first **electromagnets** and **electric motors**.

Amazing facts

- The Earth's **magnetic field** has flipped direction many times in the past. In just a thousand years or so, the strength of the field falls to zero, and then builds up again in the opposite direction. The last time the Earth's north and south magnetic poles swapped places was about 700,000 years ago.

- Everything has some magnetism, but in the case of most objects it is millions of times weaker than the magnetism of **compass needles** and similar objects. This means that most things are affected by magnetic fields by a very small amount. Dutch scientists have been able to make objects levitate (float in the air) using very strong magnetic fields. They have done this with drops of water, vegetables and even a living frog – which was unharmed.

- A **magnet** falls more slowly through a metal tube than a non-magnetic object does. As the magnet falls, each part of the metal tube 'feels' the strength of its magnetic field changing. This changing field disturbs the **electrons** in the **atoms** of the metal, and sets up **electric currents** in the metal. These currents have magnetism that acts on the magnet, slowing it down.

29

►• Glossary

aluminium light silvery metal that is not magnetic

atom one of the small particles that matter is made of. An atom is made of smaller particles, including electrons.

attract/attraction pull without touching, as a magnet pulls metal objects, and the Earth pulls objects down towards itself

aurora area of glowing coloured light in the sky, most often seen in the far north and south

battery device that generates electric current by a chemical reaction

circuit arrangement of electrical components through which current can flow to do some job

compass needle light thin bar magnet used in a magnetic compass

crystal type of material in which the atoms are arranged in an orderly pattern

diaphragm thin plate of material, such as metal or plastic. A vibrating diaphragm is important in a loudspeaker.

domain tiny region of a material in which all the atoms are pointing the same way, so that their magnetic fields add together

electric current stream of electrons or other particles. The current has a magnetic field, and can produce heat or light.

electric motor machine that uses electric current to produce motion

electromagnet device that develops a magnetic field when electric current is passed through it

electron particle found in every atom. Most electric current is a flow of electrons.

force influence that alters or moves an object

generator machine for producing an electric current. It is usually driven by steam.

hemisphere half of a sphere, or globe, especially of the Earth

lodestone natural magnet

loudspeaker device that produces sound using the electric current from a radio, TV set, telephone or other such device

maglev abbreviation for 'magnetic levitation' – 'levitation' means 'lifting'. Maglev vehicles are lifted above a track by the force between electromagnets in the vehicle and in the track.

magnet object that can attract certain metals, such as iron

magnetic describes a material that either is, or can be made into, a magnet

magnetic compass device containing a light magnetized rod, or 'needle', that is free to turn to point towards the Earth's magnetic poles

magnetic field pattern of magnetic influence around a magnet

magnetic field lines imaginary lines that show the direction of a magnetic field at each point in space

magnetic pole part of a magnet where the magnetic field is strongest

magnetic tape plastic tape coated with magnetic metal, for recording sounds, TV pictures or computer data

magnetize to turn an object made of magnetic material into a magnet

microphone device that detects sounds and produces an electric current, which can be used to produce copies of the original sounds at another time or place

migrate/migration regular movement of animals in search of food or breeding places

molten melted and at high temperature

motor machine that produces motion – either from electricity or by burning a fuel such as petrol

particle very small piece of matter

power station plant where electrical power is produced

repel push away, often without touching – similar poles of different magnets repel each other

rotor rotating coil in an electric motor or generator

substation place where transformers alter the voltage of electricity – for example, reducing it to make it safer to use in the home

transformer device for altering electrical voltage

vibration rapid backwards-and-forwards motion

voltage 'push' that makes electric current flow

▶• Index

▶• More books to read

Science Fact Files: Electricity and Magnetism, Steve Parker (Hodder Wayland, 2001)
Science in Our World: Electricity and Magnetism, Brian J Knapp (Atlantic Europe Publishing Co Ltd, 1991)
Science Topics: Electricity and Magnetism, Anne Fullick and Chris Oxlade (Heinemann Library, 2000)
Hands on Science: Magnets to Dynamos: Projects with Magnetism, Peter Lafferty (Franklin Watts, 1989)